GE   DON

Anita Ganeri and

Beatriz Castro

W
FRANKLIN WATTS

First published in Great Britain in 2023
by Hodder and Stoughton
Copyright © Hodder and Stoughton
Limited, 2023

Credits
Series editor: Julia Bird
Illustrator: Beatriz Castro
Design: Collaborate

HB: 978 1 4451 8219 3
PB: 978 1 4451 8220 9

Franklin Watts
An imprint of Hachette Children's Group
Part of Hodder and Stoughton
Carmelite House
50 Victoria Embankment
London EC4Y 0DZ

An Hachette UK company.
www.hachette.co.uk
www.hachettechildrens.co.uk

Printed in Dubai

GET BETTER SOON

Cold

Hello there. My name's Roshan, and this book is all about the time I caught a cold. I felt really rubbish. My nose was all blocked up. I had a sore throat, and I couldn't stop sneezing. But after a few days' rest, I felt much better.

This book has lots of information and advice about catching a cold to help you, and your parents or carers. On the following pages, you can find out:

What is a cold?

How do you catch one?

Why does a cold make you sneeze?

What makes you feel better?

This book is about an illness, called the common cold.
You might catch three or more colds a year.
And you're not alone. At any time, millions of people
around the world have got a cold!

It's Thursday morning. Roshan and his friends are standing outside school. Today's the day of the school trip to the science museum. They are waiting for the coach.

Is that the coach? Over there?

I can't see it. I hope we're not going to be late.

The children have been looking forward to this trip for weeks. They all start talking about what they want to see.

I want to see the dinosaur bones. What about you, Roshan?

I can't wait to see the space rocks.

I like, *sniff*, planes, *sniff*.

A few minutes later, the coach drives into the car park.
The children's chatter gets louder and louder.
Miss Lindsay, the class teacher, claps her hands.

Quiet, everyone! Now, find your partner, and get into a nice queue.

Miss Lindsay, and her teaching assistant, Mr Balik, tick off the children as they climb on board the coach.

Roshan is queuing up with his partner,
Poppy. He isn't feeling very well.
He has a sore throat and a headache.

Are you okay, Roshan?
You're not your usual
chatty self.

I'm fine, thanks.
I'm just excited about
the trip.

Glad to hear it!
Now, is anyone missing?

At the science museum, the children are amazed by all the different things on display.

In the space display, Tom spots a space suit.

Wow! This suit was worn by a real-life astronaut!

Sophia rushes straight to the dinosaurs.

I wouldn't even reach this dinosaur's knee!

Fetch!

Maya is busy playing with a robot dog.

Meanwhile, Roshan heads towards the flight simulator, where he can pretend to fly a jet.

This was meant to be the best bit of the trip. Roshan wants to be a pilot when he grows up. But his headache is getting worse, and his legs are aching. He decides to sit down for a moment.

11

Then Roshan hears Miss Lindsay's voice.

The class gather around Miss Lindsay. She points to a display about germs.

Class, can you all come here? There's something I want to see.

Right, can anyone tell me what a germ is?

Errr ...

Well, luckily, we've come to the right place to find out!

Some facts about germs ...

Germs are so tiny you need a microscope to see them.

Germs are everywhere – in the air, in the soil, and on the things around you.

The smallest germs are called viruses.

There are thousands of different kinds of germ.

Your body usually fights germs off, but sometimes, they make you ill.

Viruses can get inside your body through your eyes, nose or mouth.

Here are some of the illnesses which are caused by viruses:

COMMON COLD

* A common illness of your nose and throat
* Spread by air in tiny droplets
* Symptoms include: coughing; sneezing; sore throat

INFLUENZA

* A more serious illness, also known as the 'flu', for short
* Spread by air in tiny droplets
* Symptoms include: fever; muscle aches; feeling exhausted

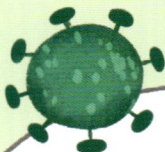

CHICKENPOX

* A common illness, often caught during childhood
* Spread by air in tiny droplets.
* Symptoms include: fever; itchy spots on the skin

COVID-19

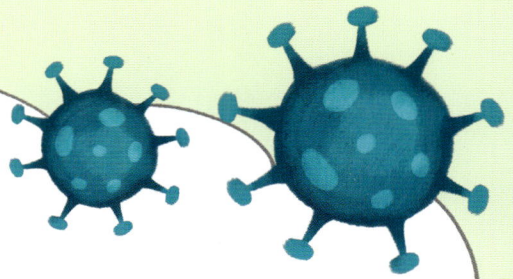

* A serious new disease
* Spread through the air and by touching contaminated surfaces
* Symptoms include: a continuous cough, high temperature and loss or change to sense of taste and smell.

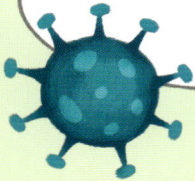

VACCINES

Vaccines are medicines that help stop you getting infections.

When you get a vaccine, it teaches your body how to fight off the germ. If the germ tries to infect you later, your body is ready to fight it off before it makes you ill.

Every year, vaccines save millions of lives around the world.

Later, back at school, the class settle down at their tables. Roshan is feeling very sleepy. He's finding it difficult to concentrate.

Suddenly, there's a loud noise ...

Roshan has done a great big snotty sneeze!

The children sitting nearby quickly lean away from poor Roshan, but Mr Balik smiles sympathetically.

Roshan finally gets it – he's caught a cold!

Roshan, would you like a tissue?

COLD CLUES

Colds are very common illnesses. Adults can catch around 2-3 colds a year; children may catch even more. Right now, millions of people around the world have got a cold!

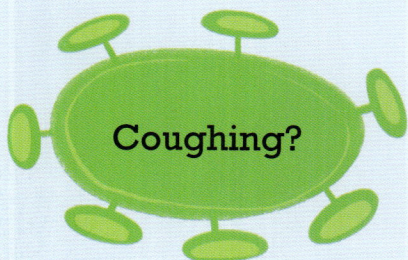

Blocked-up or runny nose?

Coughing?

But how do you know if you've got a cold?
Here are some clues to look out for:

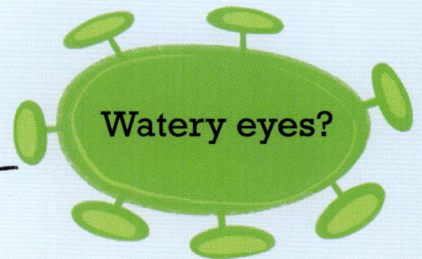

Feeling tired?

Watery eyes?

Sneezing?

Sore throat?

If you've got some or all of these, you've probably got a cold. Don't worry, you should be feeling better soon.

DID YOU KNOW?

The changes you notice in your body when you're ill are called symptoms. They show that your body is fighting the disease. This uses up a lot of energy which is why you feel tired.

Coughing and sneezing are two of the main symptoms of a cold.

Here are some things you might not know about colds and their symptoms:

Cold germs get inside your nose and throat.

The germs make your nose and throat swollen and sore.

Your body makes slimy mucus to trap the germs.

But the mucus and swelling block up your breathing tubes.

You sneeze and cough to try to clear the blockages.

A-A-A-CHOOO!

When you sneeze or cough, you blast thousands of tiny droplets of mucus into the air. If other people breathe these droplets in, they could catch the cold too.

Catch a sneeze in a tissue or cover your mouth when you cough. That will help to stop the germs from spreading.

21

Roshan's dad comes to pick him up at the end of school. Roshan is sneezing a lot now. His throat is sore, and he keeps coughing.

How are you feeling buddy?

Not good!

Back home, Dad sends Roshan straight to bed.

Later, he brings Roshan his favourite spicy soup. But Roshan can't taste very much.

Get some rest, Roshan. I'll check on you later.

TOP TIPS

A cold is usually a mild illness, and you don't need to see a doctor. But there are some things that can help you feel better:

1. Get plenty of rest.
2. Keep warm.
3. Drink plenty of water.
4. Eat small amounts of soup, or other food that is easy to swallow.

DID YOU KNOW?

While you have a cold, you are infectious. This means that you can easily spread your germs to other people. You can start spreading a cold a few days before you get any symptoms. You're infectious until all your symptoms have gone.

Here are some things you can do to stop your cold spreading, and to stop yourself catching a cold from someone else:

Wash your hands often with soap and warm water.

Catch the germs in a tissue when you cough or sneeze.

Put any used tissues in the bin.

Don't share towels or things like mugs.

Try not to touch your eyes or nose!

The next morning, Roshan is feeling a bit better.
But he's still coughing and keeps blowing his nose.

You should stay off school today. It's Friday so you'll have the weekend to rest up.

Okay - *sniff* - Dad!

By Monday, Roshan's feeling much better.
He can't wait to go back to school and see his
friends. He packs plenty of tissues in his bag.

In the classroom, Roshan looks around for Tom.
He can't see him anywhere. He asks Mr Balik
if he knows where Tom is.

Tom's not coming to school today. His mum says he's caught a cold!

Oh no!

QUIZ

Now you've reached the end of the book, how much do you think you know about colds? Try this quick quiz to find out.

1. What causes a cold?
a) Viruses
b) Germs
c) Cold weather

2. Which of these are signs of a cold?
a) Sneezing
b) Coughing
c) Runny nose

3. Which of these will stop your cold spreading?
a) Sharing things like mugs and towels
b) Having dirty hands
c) Blowing your nose into a tissue

4. Which of these will help you feel better?
a) Running around
b) Jumping up and down
c) Getting plenty of rest

5. When can you go back to school?
a) After a week
b) After a month
c) When your symptoms have gone

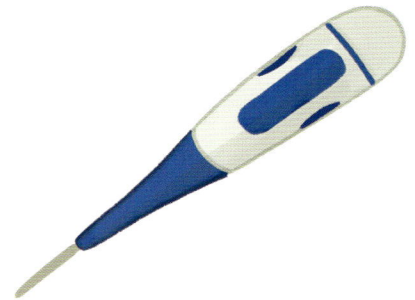

Answers:
1. a); 2. All of them; 3. c); 4. c); 5. c)

USEFUL WORDS

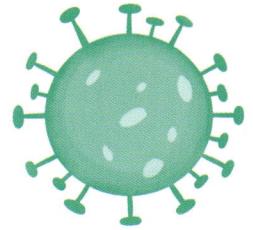

Contaminated
Something that has germs on it.

Droplets
Tiny drops of liquid.

Germs
Tiny living things that can
cause disease.

Infectious
Disease that can be caught by
being close to someone who has it.

Microscope
Scientific instrument used to make
tiny objects look bigger.

Mucus
Thick liquid made by your
nose; also called snot.

Sympathetically
In a kind and understanding way.

Symptoms
Signs of an illness.

Vaccines
Medicines usually given by injection
to stop you getting a disease.

Viruses
Types of germ that can get inside your
body and make you ill.

MORE INFORMATION

www.kidshealth.org/en/kids/colds.html
More information about catching a cold, and how to feel better.

www.kids.britannica.com/kids/article/Common-Cold/400001
Learn more about catching a cold, and how it affects your body.

BOOKS

Health and My Body: The Common Cold by Beth Bence Reinke
(Pebble Books, 2021)

Tiny Science: Germs by Anna Claybourne (Wayland, 2021)

*The Secret Life of Viruses: Incredible Science Facts About Germs,
Vaccines and What You Can Do to Stay Healthy* by Mariona Tolosa
Sisteré (Sourcebooks, 2021)

ADVICE FOR PARENTS AND CARERS

Colds and flu start off with many of the same symptoms, which makes them difficult to tell apart. But flu is more serious than a cold, and can make your child feel really ill.

Here are some signs to look out for to tell them apart:

COLD

- A cold usually appears slowly, over a few days.

- A cold may give your child a slightly raised temperature.

- A cold can make your child feel unwell, but they may be able to carry on as normal.

- A cold mainly affects your child's nose and throat.

FLU

- Flu can come on quickly, maybe in a few hours.

- Flu can give a sudden high temperature (of 38°C or above).

- Flu may make your child feel so ill and exhausted that they have to stop.

- Flu also affects their nose and throat, but they may also have a headache, earache, tummy ache, aching muscles and feel sick.

If you think that your child has flu, follow the tips for treating a cold (see page 23). Call your doctor if you're worried about your child or if their temperature lasts for five days or more and doesn't come down with paracetamol.

You can also ask for advice from your chemist.

All children at primary school in the UK are offered an annual nasal spray flu vaccine.

INDEX

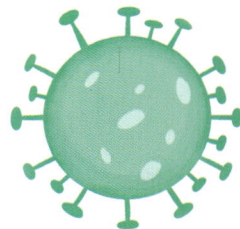